IMAGES OF ENGLAND

LITTLEHAMPTON
REVISITED

IMAGES OF ENGLAND

LITTLEHAMPTON
REVISITED

ROLF ZEEGERS, JULIET NYE
AND LUCY ASHBY

The
History
Press

Frontispiece: Littlehampton Harbour, 1900.

First published in 2007

Reprinted in 2011 by
The History Press
The Mill, Brimscombe Port,
Stroud, Gloucestershire, GL5 2QG
www.thehistorypress.co.uk

Reprinted 2013

British Library Cataloguing in Publication Data.
A catalogue record for this book is available from the British Library.

ISBN 978 0 7524 3987 7

Typesetting and origination by Tempus Publishing Limited.
Printed in Great Britain.

Contents

Acknowledgements

The authors would like to thank Sidney Fogg and Victoria Lappin for their assistance in completing this book.

Special thanks go to Littlehampton Town Council for giving permission to use the Museum's Photographic Archive.

All of the photographs used in this book have come from the Littlehampton Museum Archive. We would like to thank the following people who donated photographs to Littlehampton Museum which have been used in this book: Mr T. Attle, Mr R. Burchfield, Mrs Calcutt, Mr E.R. Collings, Mrs P. Cowles, Mr A. Creese, Mrs I. Doble, Mrs P.H. Dotts, Mr R. Elleray, Mr R. Fitzgerald, Mr A. Floyd, Mr H. Ford, Mrs J. Fordharm, Mrs B. Greenshields, Mr Hammond, Mrs Hardy, Mrs A. Hawkins, Mrs J. Haynes, Mr Humphrey, Mrs J. Izatt, Mr M. Jennings, Mr C. Joiner, Ms B. Jones, Ms I. Jones, Mr Jones, Mr N.C. Landridge, Mr M. Langley, Mrs D. Legg, Mrs Y. Lewis, Mr F. Licence, Littlehampton Local History Society, Mrs Marshall, Mr C. Nairn, Mr A. Richmond, Mrs A. Robinson, Mr S. Robinson, Rosemead Educational Trust, Mrs Smart, Miss B. Staff, Ms D. Stanford, Mr Spooner, Mrs Spry, Mr T. Squires, Mrs Swewin, Mr J. Thompson, Major F. Townsend, Mr Tubb, Mrs K. Turner, Mrs P. Turrell, Mrs Vowles, Mr T. Wales.

We apologise if, despite our best efforts, a copyright photograph has been used inadvertently or a donor has not been acknowledged.

Introduction

Our aim for this publication has been to paint a picture of life in Littlehampton for the community as captured by local photographers. We hope that the readers enjoy exploring the colourful and fascinating past of their ancestors as much as we have enjoyed our journey uncovering the stories included within this special book.

The material focuses on local people and daily life in Littlehampton as shown in our archive photographs at Littlehampton Museum. The chapters concentrate on the personal aspects of the lives of those who walked the streets of Littlehampton many years ago. Their lives were much the same as ours are today, going to school, doing their shopping, visiting the fair and relaxing on the beach.

The majority of the collection has been generously donated over the years by the public, along with museum purchases made to enrich the already impressive range of images. The archive consists of over 10,000 photographs and slides, ranging from the mid-nineteenth century to the present day. The collection features a record of shops and businesses in the district, the area before it was developed into the busy residential and commercial centre we see today, and most importantly we have a unique insight into the characters that formed our town.

This book is dedicated to all the people who have generously donated images to Littlehampton Museum over the years, and who have made this book possible.

The Littlehampton Story

Littlehampton is located on the coastal plain below the South Downs and alongside the river Arun. It has always been a popular area to live, with evidence of human activity going back to prehistoric and Roman times. Littlehampton first appears written as 'Hantone' in the Domesday Book of AD1086. A waxen thermograph map from Carentan in France from around AD1100 shows Littlehampton as a small fishing community. The area was owned by the Earls of Arundel and later the Dukes of Norfolk who still live at Arundel. Littlehampton started to develop as a port due to constant silting of the river Arun making it less navigable for larger ships. In 1735 a new river-mouth channel was cut and a wooden harbour erected at Littlehampton. By the late Middle Ages, the town had changed its name to 'Littlehampton' in order to distinguish it from Southampton further along the South Coast.

The town started to develop from a fishing community to a holiday resort from the late eighteenth century. The relaxed and tranquil location attracted famous painters and poets such as Byron, Coleridge, Shelley and Constable. With the threat of foreign invasion a gun battery was built on the East Bank guarding the mouth of the river Arun by 1760. A later fort was built on the west beach side in 1854.

Expansion and growth of Littlehampton continued in the nineteenth century. In 1801 the population stood at 584 and by 1901 it had increased to 5,954. The development of trade from fishing to ship building and importing of aggregates and Baltic wood played a major part in the town's economic success. However, it was the holiday trade, the building of a direct train route into the town, and having a cross-channel ferry service to Honfleur in France in the latter half of the nineteenth century that made the town prosperous as a Victorian holiday resort.

This trend continued well into the twentieth century with holiday seasons in Littlehampton. By the late 1920s the town was known as 'The Children's Paradise'. Post-war brought further changes with the building of new housing estates on the outskirts and absorbing surrounding villages like Wick, Lyminister and Toddington. Trade altered to light industry such as boat building and water sports. However, Littlehampton continued to attract holiday makers and is a well-established holiday resort on the South Coast.

Today Littlehampton has around 30,000 inhabitants and is slowly reinventing itself as a holiday resort for the twenty-first century. Change is already on the way to ensure Littlehampton's future as a premier destination on the South Coast. New café facilities on east beach and the redevelopment of the riverside area has done much to improve the look of the once-celebrated resort. Its long stretch of beach front and beautiful nineteenth-century architecture instils pride in its inhabitants and the town is popular with holidaymakers the world over.

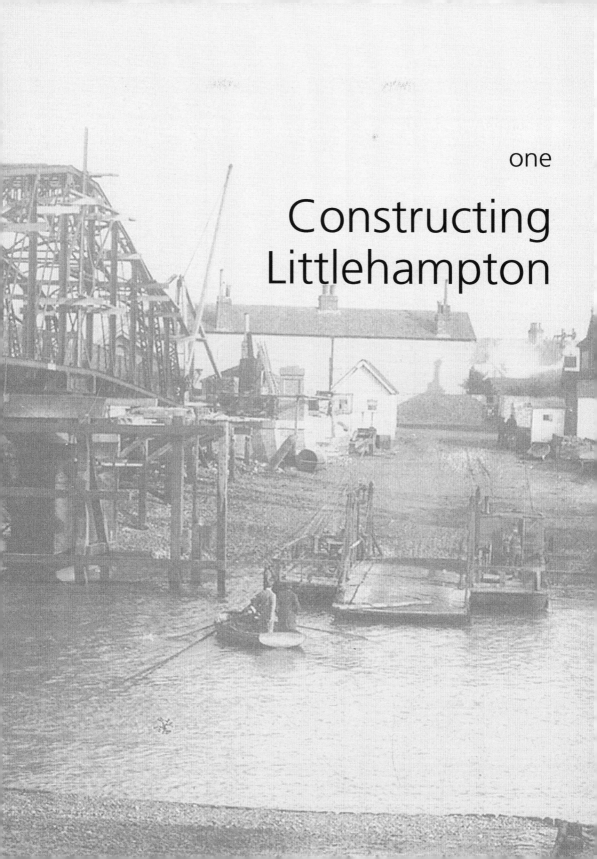

one

Constructing
Littlehampton

Littlehampton Waterworks. The water tower was built in 1881 by Grantham & Son Engineers. The 91ft tower stood in St Flora's Road and remained in use until 1952 before being demolished in 1961. The water tower supplied the town's water for some eighty years.

The laying of the library foundation stone by Lord Talbot MP on 4 March 1905. The building was situated in Maltravers Road and was financed by American philanthropist Andrew Carnegie. The public library opened on 30 May 1906. The first appointed librarian was Mr W.H. Nagle.

Littlehampton and District Hospital.

Littlehampton Hospital situated in Fitzalan Road opened on 22 August 1911. The building was built entirely from donations including the land which was given as a gift by Henry Fitzalan–Howard, fifteenth Duke of Norfolk. The hospital cost £1,600 to build and was designed by the architects Frederick Wheeler and C.R.B. Godman of Horsham. An X–ray room was added in 1916.

Building the blue–coloured giant dipper at Butlins Amusement Park in 1936. Billy Butlin bought the Arun Mill and Coastguard Cottages site near the seafront in 1931. In 1933 he opened his amusement park after redevelopment of the site and it became a popular tourist attraction.

Trial borings for the swing bridge in April 1906. Duke & Ockendens Engineers carried out the borings and laid the foundations of the bridge. The company was founded in 1887 and were experts in laying and constructing water supply systems.

Construction of the swing bridge in 1907. It was built by the firm Alfred Thorne & Sons of Westminster and designed by J.J. Webster. The bridge cost £26,000 to build.

First horses over the swing bridge in April 1908. The bridge took two years to build and the decision to build it had been decided by a local referendum on 13 January 1905. A total of 888 people voted and the result was 675 in favour of the bridge and 213 against it.

First car over the swing bridge in April 1908. The car was driven by Neville Perrin Edwards. On 7 August 1907 Henry Fitzalan-Howard, fifteenth Duke of Norfolk, laid the bridge's foundation stone. The official opening ceremony of the swing bridge took place on 27 May 1908. The event was celebrated by the town.

The old chain ferry and new swing bridge in 1908. The chain ferry was built in Thomas Isemonger's shipyard in 1824 and started its service in June 1825. It was replaced by an iron ferry in 1870. The ferry provided transport across the river Arun for eighty-three years. It was eventually sold for £40 and was converted into a houseboat.

Building the Arun Riverside Parade in 1928. In 1873, the old east jetty was rebuilt into the pier. A proposal to build a new riverside parade was considered in 1914 but not implemented until fourteen years later.

Building the Arun Riverside Parade from West Beach in 1928. The lighthouses were built in 1848 and were known as the Salt and Pepper Pots. They were a main feature of the town up until the Second World War when they were demolished for identification reasons.

Workmen involved in building the Arun Riverside Parade in 1928. The man holding the adze was Charles Dutton.

Building the Arcade in 1922. The site had been Martin Eagle grocery store. Other businesses that had previously occupied the site included a smithy and ironmongery shop owned by William Ockenden in the mid-1850s.

A new post office built in the Arcade in 1922. With the advent of stamps and the popularity of sending letters, a more centrally based postal depot was required in the town.

The interior of the new post office in 1922. Today the post office is still in the same location. The war memorial in the post office commemorates fallen office workers, John Abraham Carpenter from the First World War and Edward William George Rosam and George Albert Mundy from the Second World War.

Laying of a sewer in Wick Street in 1898. The pipes were laid by Duke & Ockenden Water Supply Engineers. The council debated the benefits of installing a sewer in Wick. It was installed in the interest of health reasons. Vine Cottage, built in 1888, is on the left.

Ships being built at Harvey's Shipyard at the beginning of the twentieth century. This shipyard was taken over by Henry Harvey in 1848. Henry Harvey was originally from Rye where he had a small shipyard. The yard mainly built wooden sailing ships and barges. John and William Harvey took over the business after Henry's death in 1868.

Harvey's Shipyard ceased to operate in 1921 and the site was taken over by other boat-building firms.

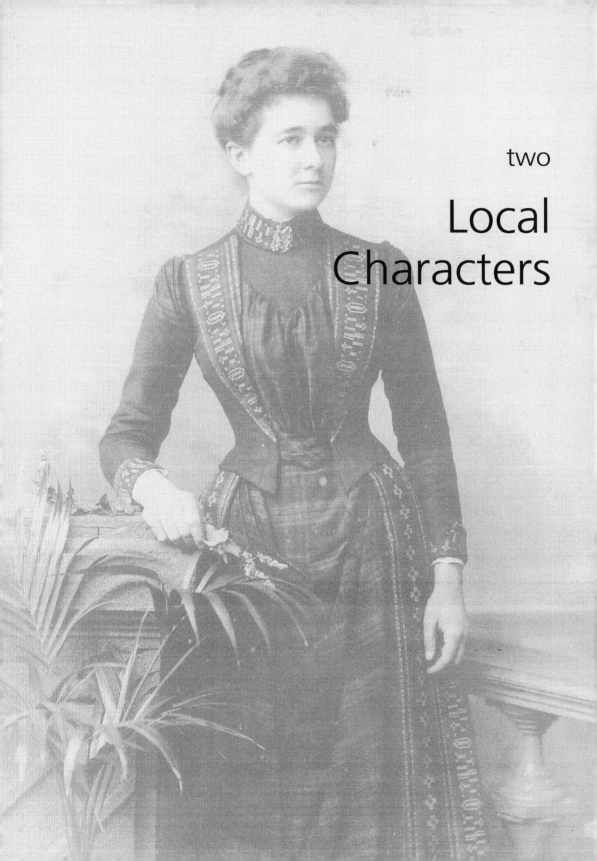

two

Local
Characters

Mr Fred Spencer. 'Freddie' Spencer used to entertain the crowds at Littlehampton with his variety performances during the early twentieth century. Children and adults alike loved his impersonations and costumes. His repertoire included singing such songs as 'I have knitted myself a jumper'.

Freddie Spencer in costume as Mrs 'Arris of the Sunday 'Erald, 1924.

Harry Joseph and his company of performers
began entertaining Littlehampton audiences in
1892. During the winter, theatrical productions
were put on in The Victoria Hall in New Road,
and throughout the summer Pierrot shows were
staged on the Green.

Mr Harry Joseph, *c.* 1910.

Left: Miss Lena Joseph, *c.* 1910. Harry's daughter Lena used to perform with the troupe each summer when she returned home from boarding school.

Below: Harry Joseph's Pierrots against the Beach Hotel wall, *c.* 1900. In 1912 Joseph's Pierrot Troupe won the 'All-England Pierrot Contest' at the London Palladium after receiving nearly 20,000 votes.

Dr White Eye's Minstrel Group taken by local photographer Frank Spry. Dr White Eye, whose real name was Stephens, and his troupe were very popular with children. They performed at various locations around Littlehampton during the 1920s, the most common being the first groyne, then known as the 'free' groyne, by the pier.

A branch of the Robinson family. From left to right: Kathleen, Mary Jane (née Burt), Reg (standing), Joseph Edward, Joseph Richard, Alex (seated in front).

The Robinsons were a prominent shipping family in Littlehampton for much of the nineteenth and early twentieth century. Joseph Edward was master of the ship *Atossa* which was given up for lost when, on 27 August 1883, the ship and its crew were caught up in the vicinity of Krakatoa when it erupted, killing more than 36,000 people. On Joseph's orders, however, the crew had climbed upon the masts and rigging thus surviving unharmed to tell the tale. This picture was taken to on 15 September 1914, to celebrate the eldest son Joseph Richard's twenty-first birthday.

Maurice Edmund Robinson, 1862–1936. Like most of his family, Captain Robinson spent some of his working life as a ship's master. In 1898 he accompanied his brothers, Arthur and Sidney, to Klondyke, Canada, with the notion of becoming gold prospectors. Upon reaching their destination Maurice and his brothers parted company and he joined forces with another prospector. This partnership, however, was short lived with Maurice soon losing his temper and sawing in half the boat that they shared!

Louis Robinson. Louis began his seafaring career as an apprentice on board the *Trossachs*. This was the largest ship ever built in Littlehampton. From 1902 to 1915 he was master of the *Ebenezer*, the last ship belonging to the port of Littlehampton. Upon his retirement Louis became well known as a local fisherman.

Margaret Louise Haywood, known as Peggy, 1871–1964. Peggy owned a boarding house at 131 Victoria Terrace where she was landlady to Mrs Blackbourne. Mrs Blackbourne came from Eastbourne and was a regular visitor to Littlehampton from 1895 to 1917. She was a non-professional cartoonist who was inspired by local stories, drawing what she saw in her individual and unique style. Her album contains over 140 watercolour sketches showing life in Littlehampton at the beginning of the twentieth century.

Left: Mrs Blackbourne, self portrait.

Opposite above: Mrs Blackbourne's husband-hunting Harris sisters can be seen in this image taken at a benefit afternoon on 19 August 1908. They are seated in the third row, in between two sets of children. Reginald Robinson can also be seen in the front row, wearing a cap.

'The Harris Sisters' by Mrs Blackbourne. The Harris sisters appear to have caught Mrs Blackbourne's eye during their husband hunt at the seaside.

Dr John H. Candy. Dr Candy was one of
Littlehampton's leading physicians during
the nineteenth century. Having practised
medicine since 1820, he went on to become
the first chairman of the Littlehampton Board
of Health in 1855, staying in post for three
years and serving again from 1865 to 1878.
The Board of Health was replaced in 1894 by
the Arun Urban District Council. Dr Candy
lived for a time in The Manor House where
the current Town Council and the Museum
are located.

Molly Gray. Molly owned a cottage at the top
of Arundel Road where she made and sold
an exciting range of sweets to local children
and adults. Her window was said to have been
full of different types of lollypops and chews,
which she sold in batches of eight or fourteen
for a penny. Even the various sailors travelling
to and fro used to remember 'Old Molly' and
popped in for their sweets whenever they
stopped at Littlehampton. Molly's cottage was
demolished in 1905 when Clun Road was
built.

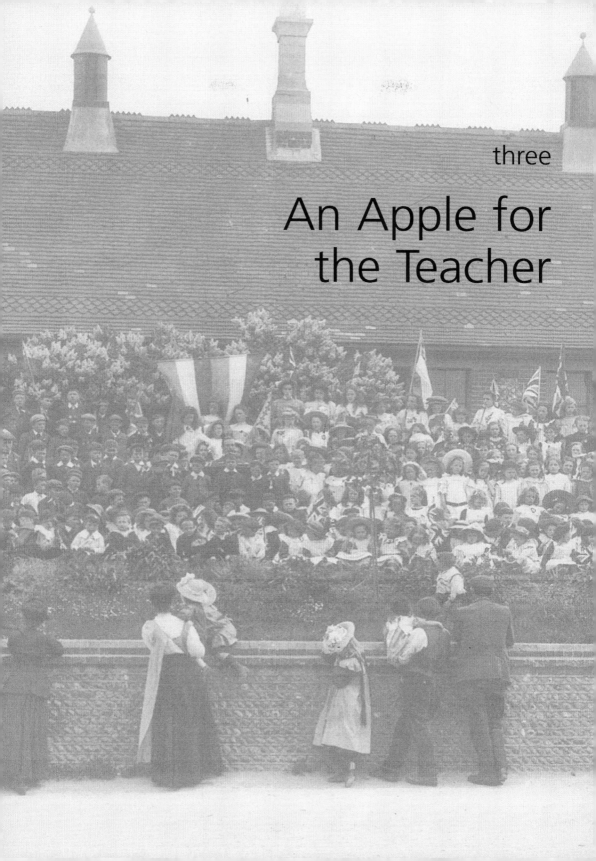

three

An Apple for the Teacher

A view of Surrey House, *c.* 1870. The school was built in 1790 by the fifth Earl of Berkeley on Littlehampton seafront. It was run as a school until 1885 by John Grix and later George Neame. It then became a hotel, and was pulled down in 1948.

Children from Clymping School in the 1920s. The present school buildings were once known as Clymping Mill, which dates to 1799. An inscription was dedicated to 'Letitia Matilda Walsh, mistress of Clymping School 1878–1921' at Clymping church.

Sports day at Hadleigh House School, c. 1910. There was a great increase in the number of private schools during the Victorian period. At one time there were forty-one registered institutions. Hadleigh House School was situated in Western Road and the headmaster in 1903 was Sidney H. Poole.

Schoolchildren in costume at a summer fête on Littlehampton Sports Field in the 1920s.

Groombridge House School girls in the 1920s. From left to right, back row: J.Briggs, P. Lindfield, D. Brown, M. Hayward, E. Searl, G. Cartwright, I. Westbrook. Second row: C. Douglass, P. Potter, I. Ockenden, B. Brooks, W. Hayward, E. Bergstrom, C. Reynolds, L. Draper. Third row: M. Warrell, –?–, M. Elliot, W. Tucker, D. Wallis, I. Rickards, I. Westbrook, –?–, V. Hopkins, M. Wheaton. Bottom row: L. Walsh, Cartwright, –?–, P. Blanchard, Mymie Warrell, K. Harris, Isobel Rickards, M. Cretchly, ? Cartwright, L. Bignal, P. Wheaton, D. Blanchard.

Spectre Drill at Groombridge House School in the 1920s. From left to right, back row: N. Brooks, D. Brown, I. Ockenden, ? Lough. Second row: Gladys Cartwright, C. Douglas, M. Hayward. Front row: Mavis Warrell, Dulcy Wallis, M. Wheaton.

Groombridge girls, *c.* 1915. The principal at this time was J.W.C. Langfield and the premises were situated at 23 South Terrace. From left to right, back row: Majory Stacey, Phyllis Gates, Eileen Redman. Middle row: Lilian Plant-Hollins, Ivy Ockenden, Majory Stone. Bottom Row: Molly Gibbs, Doris Merton, Jose Briggs.

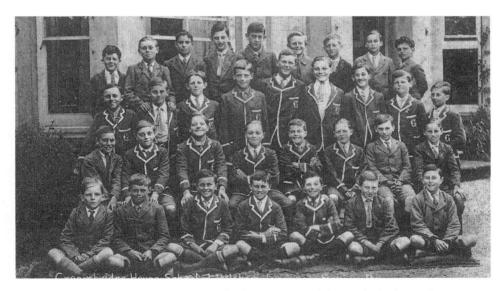

The senior boys of Groombridge House School, *c.* 1915. From left to right, back row: Reggy Sparks, G. Walshaw, C. Tidy, G. Brown, ? Gardner, G. Wild, Briggs, O. Beaumont, E. Stringer. Second row: C. Powell, –?–, –?–, E. Wright, D. Campbell, E. Andre, D. Goode, J. Harris, R. Harrison. Third row: Walshaw, E. Cocksedge, ? Scroogie, A. Rumsey, –?–, ? Rumsey, G. Campbell, W. Barges. Bottom Row: D. Geneley, Jaycock, D. Draper, –?–, F. Holland, –?–, G. Thomson.

Marjory Stacey and her classmates from Groombridge House School, enjoying a day out to celebrate 'Peace' on the river Arun, *c.* 1918. They hired a boat named *Norfolk* and sailed up to Arundel where they had lunch at the Black Rabbit.

School children from East Street School, Littlehampton. The school was opened in 1878 as a boarding school and later became a girls' school run by headmistress and local woman Miss E. Boniface.

Wick school children outside their school building, *c.* 1905. Wick School (now Lyminster County Infants) was built as result of the 1870 Education Act, which saw the Government contributing to state education and ensuring that children received a free education.

East Street School (now the Flintstone Centre).

The staff of East Street School in the 1920s. Pictured in the centre wearing a necklace is Miss E. Boniface.

Class No. 2 of East Street Girls' School, with headmistress Miss E. Boniface pictured on the far left, *c.* 1910.

Evacuees from Littlehampton to Radcliffe-on-Trent. In the Second World War the town was filled with evacuees from London, and Littlehampton schools had to share their buildings with them. By 1940 it was the turn of local children to be evacuated to the Midlands, and the population of Littlehampton decreased from 13,800 to 9,800.

Children from Wick School taking part in a parade to celebrate the opening of the swing bridge on 27 May 1908. The whole town took part in the event, and a tea party was held by the river Arun for the children of Littlehampton.

The Wick school children walking along Wick Street with their Union Jacks flying. They were taking part in the procession down to the river Arun to mark the opening of the swing bridge in 1908.

Opposite above: Front view of Rosemead School in the 1960s. Rosemead Girls' School was founded by Miss Sharpe and Miss Young in 1919. By the 1960s it had become a public school, and a new science block and senior girls' wing had been added. The school celebrated its golden jubilee in 1969, and at that time they had 160 boarders aged eleven to eighteen. Rosemead closed in 1995 and has since merged with Lavant House School in Chichester.

Opposite below: Girls from Rosemead School taking part in a science lesson in the 1960s. The renowned girls' school offered a sound preparation for exams and university, teaching sciences, modern languages and physical training. This was all set in specially adapted premises and 5 acres of land in Littlehampton.

Lyminster school children celebrating Empire Day in 1909. A special day was organised all over the British Empire to commemorate the late Queen Victoria's birthday on 24 May. The idea was to encourage the values of 'Citizenship and Empire knowledge'.

Boys from Connaught School in 1928. Ken Stilwell is seen holding the slate, with Mr Norris the principal and Mr Webster the class teacher.

BAZAAR Co

four

Going Shopping

Any
Article 6½

High Street, *c.* 1880. The thatched building is Tommy Banfield's poultry and game shop. Built by James Humphrey between 1780 and 1790, this was one of two thatched shops which stood on the High Street. Both were sadly demolished in 1889 at the end of their original leases in order to provide space for Clifton Road and a new development of shops. Before being acquired by Banfield, this shop was owned by the Dudding family who ran it as a bakery.

Opposite above: The second of the two thatched shops was owned by John Nutter, a greengrocer. This image was taken as a record of the High Street shortly before the buildings were pulled down in 1889.

Opposite below: East Street, *c.* 1910. John Nutter's father, William, was originally a ship builder. In 1863 he turned his attention to his orchard in East Street where he owned a greengrocer shop. When William died in the late 1880s John transferred his business here.

OLD LITTLEHAMPTON.

International Stores, c. 1910. Notice the all-male team of staff outside the front of this general store.

International Stores, 14 September 1921. It is interesting to see how times change; here in this post-war image you can see a mixture of both male and female staff working at the store.

High Street, *c.* 1910. General store Domestic Bazaar, seen here showing an impressive window display of crockery and household goods, stood on the site currently occupied by Bonmarché.

Broadway Market, shown here in 1927, was owned by Leonard G. Yates. Located on the corner of the Arcade, this store was a greengrocers and flower shop.

George Groom's Provision Merchants, High Street, c. 1900. This shop was built on the site of the old George Inn. When the license was transferred to a building at the bottom of Arundel Road around 1920, the sons of the former landlady, Mrs Sparks, built two shops on the site. George Groom came to Littlehampton in 1892, taking over the grocery shop from Peter Ellison, the current owner who had recently died. Groom swiftly built up his business coming to own five branches located both in the town and in Wick. Located on the first floor of his main shop was Littlehampton's first telephone exchange. This shop is now a Sainsbury's.

Right: George Groom, *c.* 1900. Groom was a prominent figure in the town; he was chairman of the Urban District Council and instrumental in campaigning for the building of the bridge to cross the Arun in 1908. Sadly he took to drink and died in 1910.

Below: The second of the two shops built by the Spark brothers. This drapers was originally run by the elder brother George. Upon his retirement in 1856, the business went through a number of different managers, namely: Messers Kenward and Stoneham, Charles Smith, the Newman Brothers, Port and Jarrett and the Tiffin Brothers. John Hussey took over the shop in 1912, until he retired in 1932. The shop is now the site of Peacocks.

Smartly Tailored
Suits for Men
of all Ages!!

Phone
293

T. SYMES & SON

Personal
Service.

BEACH ROAD, LITTLEHAMPTON

Above: Surrey Street, *c.* 1925. This corner shop has been used by many different trades; here it can be seen in its life as a tailors, owned by Fred Griffiths.

Left: Advertisement for T. Symes & Son, a tailors located in Beach Road. This advertisement featured in the 1938 *Littlehampton and District Directory*.

Opposite above: Baldry's Antique Shop, High Street, 1919. Note the rather eerie portraits in the top windows, peering out as if real people watching the passers-by!

Opposite below: High Street, *c.* 1900. Sparks & Son, successful furniture makers and estate agents, were in business on this site for many years.

BALDRY'S ANTIQUE SHOP. HIGH STREET. LITTLEHAMPTON.

High Street, *c*. 1900. Clark & Robinson's ironmongers, engineers and furnishers opened in 1895. The shop was packed full of an eclectic mix of goods, ranging from bicycles and birdcages, to ovens, spades, mangles and scrubbing brushes. On the top floor was a cycle-repair workshop.

Opposite above and below: Interior of Clark & Robinson, *c*. 1900.

Above: High Street, *c.* 1912. Burton's butcher was located at 5a on the High Street. One wonders if the meat was usually displayed out front in this way, as it cannot have looked too appealing covered in all the dust and dirt from the street!

Left: An advertisment from The Official Guide to Littlehampton, 1911.

Right: This corner shop, located at 20 River Road, was owned by Mr Edwards who can be seen here standing outside around 1920.

Below: River Road, *c.* 1900. This horse–drawn oil tanker belonged to Clark & Robinson, the ironmongers located in the High Street. It provided tea rose and white rose oils from the Anglo-American Oil Co.

Surrey Street, *c.* 1905. J. Haslett owned this 'Baking and Confectionary Establishment' at 23 Surrey Street from approximately 1890 to 1908. This image was taken by local photographer Frank Spry, who had premises at No. 21.

Surrey Street, 1910. Isaac's the butchers can be seen here on the corner of Surrey Street. Next to it is Spry's photography studio. Frank Spry was a local photographer who specialised not only in studio portraits but also recorded many local events and maritime images. He moved his premises here from East Street in 1907, remaining until the 1940s. On the left-hand corner you can see J. Haslett's corner bakery which was taken over by Mr Wood around 1908.

Spry's Studio in Surrey Street, 1927. In front is a trio of staff from Ockenden's hardware shop. They have converted one of the business's vans into a float for carnival day. Ockenden's has been part of Littlehampton since 1802, when William Ockenden established a blacksmiths in the town.

GROCERY STORES,

HIGH STREET,

LITTLEHAMPTON.

The Public are respectfully informed that, on and after FRIDAY next, the 1st November, the above STORES

Will be CLOSED at Seven o'Clock in the Evening,

Except on SATURDAYS, when they will be closed at **Nine.**

This opportunity is taken of respectfully thanking the numerous customers for the very extended patronage which has been received since the issue of a similar notice at this time last year; and by continuing to supply every article of the best quality, at the lowest possible price, an increase of such support is confidently relied on.

J. STREETER,

26th October, 1872.   PROPRIETOR.

SPECIAL NOTICES.

A considerable reduction has this week been made in the price of the best WATERFORD BACON.

The Price of Australian Meat has advanced greatly in London, but being large holders of Stock, our Price is still the same:

MUTTON, 6d. per lb.; BEEF, 7d.

JUST ARRIVED, A LARGE STOCK OF

New Raisins, Currants, Spices, Peels, Figs, &c,

Of the best Samples that can be procured.

COFFEE FRESH ROASTED EVERY WEEK,

And the full benefit of the Reduction of Duty given to the purchaser.

TEAS OF THE CHOICEST DESCRIPTIONS.

Huntley and Palmer's Biscuits.   Crosse and Blackwell's Pickles.

W. W. MITCHELL, Printer, West Sussex Gazette Office, Arundel.

A poster advertisement for J. Streeter's grocery store from 20 October 1872.

five

Sun, Sea and Sandcastles

Engraving of the Green and South Terrace, 1869. The land was levelled by order of the Duke of Norfolk in the 1880s in order to provide work for the community during a period of unemployment. This first incarnation of the promenade was built in 1867 and was popular with horse riders who rode along the coast all the way to Worthing.

A view from the pier looking east towards South Terrace, c. 1872. To the left of the pier is one of a pair of lighthouses locally known as the Salt and Pepper Pots, which had unusual domes made of copper.

An early image of the first Beach Hotel, built in 1776 by Peter Le Coq, a well known smuggler who ran it as a coffee house. Towards the late Victorian period it served as a hotel to accommodate the new influx of visitors that started to holiday at Littlehampton. The Beach Hotel quickly became known as the renowned place to stay. Next to the Beach Hotel was the Arun Mill which was pulled down in 1825.

An interesting view looking east along the Littlehampton sands of the old and new Beach Hotels side by side. The newer building was built alongside the original hotel in 1887.

A family group enjoying a donkey ride on Littlehampton beach, c. 1905. The Merretts family owned the donkeys and did a roaring trade during the summer holidays. They were kept north of Grove Corner on the common and people would choose the pony or donkey they wanted to ride. The donkeys were walked home through the town to their resting place in a field opposite the Six Bells public house in Lyminster at the end of the day.

Merretts donkeys 'waiting to welcome you' on the sands at Littlehampton, c. 1905. If you were not brave enough to ride one of the donkeys you could hire a goat carriage which was very smart, and popular with nannies with young children.

Holidaymakers gathered on Littlehampton beach in August 1909 to take part in fundraising activities on behalf of the Children's Special Service Mission. The charity held regular events to help the poor and impoverished families in the area. After the First World War the Service Mission continued to hold events for those who had lost loved ones in the conflict.

Bathing tents on Littlehampton beach in the 1920s. The portable bathing tents had replaced the earlier wheeled wooden bathing huts by 1910. They were designed to be rolled up to the sea to protect the privacy of the bather and were an attempt to segregate the sexes whilst bathing.

The bandstand on the Green at Littlehampton, c. 1910. The bandstand was located in the centre of Banjo Road. Every evening and most afternoons visitors could watch military bands or dance acts. One act was a Scottish Regiment who would perform elaborate sword dances on a Sunday afternoon. The Urban District Council used to pay £200 a week to employ a band to play, and customers would pay 'tuppence' to watch the performance from a rented deck chair.

Opposite above: A view of the Common and out to sea from the Hillyers, Littlehampton, c. 1905. The grand house on South Terrace was originally a hotel, but has since served as a boy's school run by Revd W. Philpott, and later as the 'Princess Louise Children's Hospital after the Second World War. In 1964 it was known as the 'Mary McArthur' holiday home for working women.

Opposite below: Valentine postcard from the 1930s looking east across the Green and the Marina Gardens. People often enjoyed a game of cricket on the Common in front of the new Beach Hotel. In the background is the Southlands Hotel, a first-class hotel which would have charged you 6 guineas per week to board there.

THE LAWNS AND GARDENS, LITTLEHAMPTON.

A view of west beach from the 1950s. In the 1930s chalets were erected in the dunes and café facilities were introduced. West Beach was much quieter than the East Beach, and enjoyed beautiful sand dunes and unspoilt scenery.

The Oyster Pond, *c.*1910. The pond was originally used to house local fishermen's catches. It acquired its name due to the fishermen storing oysters in the pond. There was a very active model yacht club in the town in the 1920s and they would come to the Oyster Pond and race their model ships. During the annual regatta the ferrymen and fishermen would dress up and take part in races across the pond.

Children enjoying a sandcastle competition on East Beach in the 1920s. 'Uncle Dan' used to run the competitions which the local children took very seriously, using seaweed and shells to make intricate patterns in the sand. Prizes were awarded to the winners and they would get their photograph in the local paper.

Donkeys waiting for their riders on the Green, outside Butlins amusement park in the 1950s. When Billy Butlin opened the park in 1933 he held a carnival for the local children and offered free tickets for all the rides. Despite the controversy surrounding the purchase of the land and demolishing of the old mill, Butlins played a major part in rejuvenating the beachfront and was popular with holidaymakers.

Left: Alec Reed enjoying a donkey ride on east beach in 1937. By the 1930s roving cameramen were a common sight on the beach, and they would take a photograph of you for a small fee.

Below: Harry Page, also known as 'Uncle Terry', ran stalls on the seafront during the 1930s. He sold ginger beer and ice creams and ran a quiz for the children, for which there were prizes.

Thomas and Mary Ann Smith at Littlehampton Fair, c.1906. The annual fair was held on 26 May in Surrey Street. It is one of the oldest of the chartered fairs in the country, and was a highlight of the year. By 1933 the closing down of the streets to all traffic for thirty-six hours was no longer practical, and the fair was moved to Linden Park.

Taking exercise on East Beach in the 1930s. The *Daily Express* sponsored keep-fit classes on the Common at high tide and on the sands at low tide. Physical fitness was a fashionable pastime in the 1930s and the keep-fit sessions were popular with holidaymakers.

Opposite above: A regatta on the Oyster Pond in the 1930s. Littlehampton watermen organised annual events on the river for adults, and on the lake for the children. Here we can see the 'comic policeman' capsizing, a popular character in the show put on to raise funds for the local hospital.

Opposite below: Children enjoying water sports on the Oyster Pond in the 1930s.

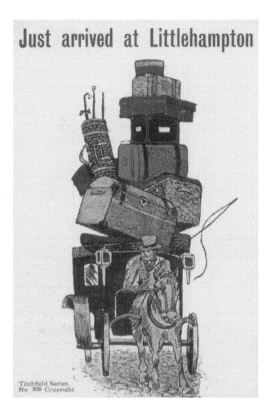

Just arrived at Littlehampton

Titchfield Series.
No. 309 Copyright

Left: A charming holiday postcard sent on 14 July 1910 to a friend in Brighton.

Below: The Littlehampton bathing pool opened in 1919 and was located on East Beach opposite Norfolk Road, but was demolished in 1939 when the lease expired. The area was enclosed in concrete so that it would fill with seawater at high tide.

THE NEW BATHING POOL, LITTLEHAMPTON

A Littlehampton postcard depicting several famous local landmarks of the town, including the old bathing pool and the Oyster Pond. It was sent by 'Auntie Gracie' on 18 August 1931, and describes her lovely afternoon in Littlehampton, but adds that she 'thought Bognor was better'!

The boating lake in the 1950s, locally known as 'Mewsbrook' after the hotel of the same name which stood on the site until 1935. In the background you can see Rustington Convalescent Home, designed by Frederick Wheeler and built in 1897.

ALL SHOULD GO FOR A TRIP
IN THE
SAFE SAILING YACHT
"SKYLARK,"
Under the management of an Experienced Sailor,
Which SAILS from the PIER EVERY DAY,
Weather and circumstances permitting, at
11 & 3 O'CLOCK.

TICKETS 1s.
AT 36, PIER ROAD, OR ON THE PIER.
C. PELHAM,
PROPRIETOR.

EVERY CLASS OF
ROWING & SMALL SAILING BOATS,
CANOES, &c.

Special Arrangements for Families.

Printed by CHILDS & Co., High Street, Littlehampton.

A flyer advertising pleasure trips aboard the *Skylark* run by C. Pelham. Boat trips were a popular pastime in the 1920s and 1930s. Tour operators provided journeys along the coast, down the river Arun and out to sea.

Holidaymakers enjoying a pleasure cruise aboard the *Lady Nancy* on 4 August 1926. This is a typical motor boat used to transport people; it was designed for safety rather than speed. Bands often sailed on the boats to provide a musical accompaniment.

Postcard sent on 4 August 1918 showing the pleasure steamers leaving and entering the harbour. Moored in the foreground is the *Jumna*, which was built in 1884 by the boatbuilding firm Hepple in Northshields. She was a much-loved tug boat which towed sailing ships out to sea between 1887 and 1923.

A view of the esplanade and green in 1915. Looking west you can see the fisherman's cottages on Pier Road and Arun Mill in the distance. The esplanade was used by holidaymakers to stroll along taking the sea air.

A typical summer scene on East Beach from the 1930s, looking west towards the pier. In the early part of the twentieth century Littlehampton was known as the 'children's paradise' with its long sandy beaches, plenty of entertainment and peace and quiet for those just wishing to relax.

six

The Impact of War

An Air Raid Precaution parade on Beach Road in 1940. Twenty-nine houses were destroyed and ninety-one houses were seriously damaged during the Second World War. A total of sixteen civilian inhabitants of the town were killed and four were declared missing.

Opposite above: A contingent of New Zealand Forces followed by the RAF marching down Beach Road during War Weapons Week in June 1941. The people of Littlehampton raised £50,000 for the War Weapons Fund.

Opposite below: 'A' Troop of the 30 Assault Unit. The 30 Assault Unit was an intelligence commando unit that was based in Littlehampton from January 1944 until January 1945. Ian Fleming, the creator of James Bond, was in charge of the unit.

The Home Guard outside East Street School in 1940. Back row, centre: R. Chapman. Middle row, third from left: C. White, fourth from left: J. Jacobs. Front row, centre: First Lieutenant M. Gosden, far right: C.C. Norris.

Opposite above: Radar pylons at Poling, north of Littlehampton, in 1940. They were 350ft in height and used to detect enemy aircraft during the Second World War. They were sold as scrap in May 1959.

Opposite below: A shot-down German Junkers 88 Bomber in the sea near Littlehampton in September 1940. The German invasion of Britain was postponed indefinitely after being defeated by the RAF in the Battle of Britain, July to October 1940.

The unloading of captured German guns on the railway wharf in 1918. Littlehampton harbour played a major role during the First World War. The majority of munitions and war stores were sent to France through this port.

Bomb crater outside the gatehouse at Rosemead School in 1941. Luckily it did not cause much damage. Rosemead School was evacuated during the Second World War. Most pupils were transferred to a mansion in Cardiganshire, Wales. Only the gatehouse remained open for day pupils throughout the war.

Bomb damage to houses in New Road. New and Maltravers Roads were bombed on 14 September 1940. One person was killed during this raid.

Bomb damage after a raid at Ford sub-station near Littlehampton on 3 October 1940. Luckily no one was injured or killed. Only the railway line and a signal box were destroyed.

Bomb damage to houses in Pier Road which was heavily bombed on 18 July 1942. Eight people were killed during the raid.

Opposite above: Crowds in Surrey Street on Armistice Day in 1918. The First World War ended of the 11 November 1918. Great Britain and her Empire lost almost 1 million men.

Opposite below: Crowds remembering the sacrifice made by the men of the town during the First World War on Armistice Day in 1930. The Armistice is remembered at 11 a.m. on the 11 November. This is the time and date that a ceasefire was implemented in the First World War.

~ LITTLEHAMPTON - NOV. 11 · 1930 ~   WHITE PHOTO.

Above: Littlehampton War Memorial.

Left: Littlehampton War Memorial was designed by the architect Edwin Lutyens. The cost for the memorial was met by subscriptions raised by the War Memorial Committee. It was unveiled on 28 September 1921 and is dedicated to the 217 men who died in the First World War. The ninety-two servicemen killed in the Second World War are also commemorated on the memorial.

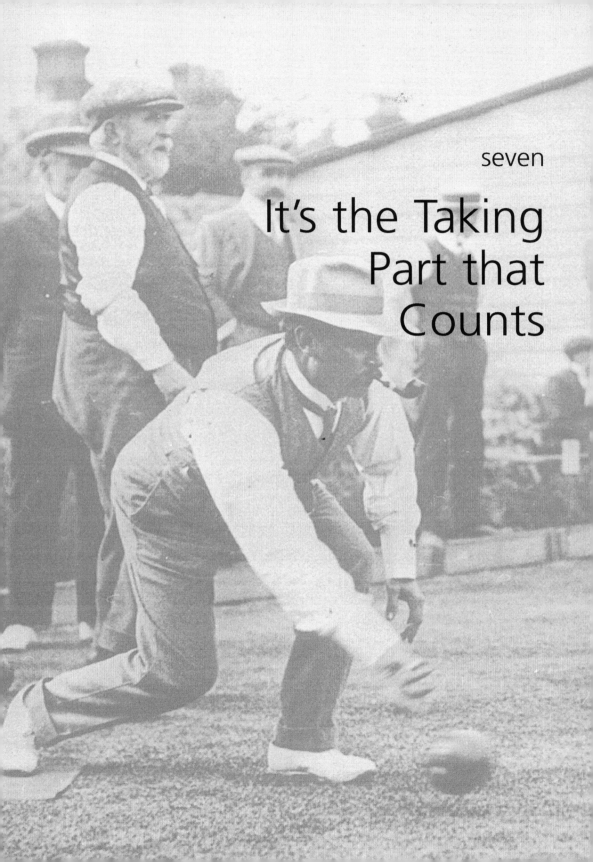

seven

It's the Taking Part that Counts

Littlehampton Lawn Tennis Club in Selbourne Place, *c.* 1900. Selbourne Place was the town's first sports field, established in the 1870s. Tournaments were held here and often attracted large numbers of people.

Opposite above: Tournament winners on the Beach Hotel tennis grounds, *c.* 1905. The ladies were required to play in full dresses which were often a hindrance, while the men would roll up their trousers and remove their caps. The referee Mr E.A.D. Blunt is the second gentleman on the left, top row.

Opposite below: Howard Lawn Tennis Club in the early twentieth century. Howard Ockenden is seated in the centre of the bottom row and his wife Edith is in the centre of the middle row. Howard Ockenden was known as a gentleman businessman and like his father, was involved in the civic life of Littlehampton, becoming chair of Littlehampton Urban District Council in 1952.

Littlehampton Amateur Athletics Club relay team in the 1930s. From left to right: Bob Cowles, Fred Hill, Dudley Bridge, Les Randall. The club trainer was Mr Stanyon and the gala meets drew thousands of spectators. During the late 1870s and early 1880s athletic sports were held annually on the August Bank Holiday. It was one of the most popular sports meetings in the south of England, and the event was managed by local resident Mr Edward Yorke of Western Road.

Sports day at Hadleigh House School playing field, c. 1915. The students discard their boaters and jackets to race for the finish line. Hadleigh House School was one of many private schools in Littlehampton during the Victorian period, and catered for the upper middle class.

Littlehampton Football Team for the 1909-10 season. The local team played their home matches on the sports field which was donated to the town in 1897. Nearby Wick had their own football club which was founded in 1891.

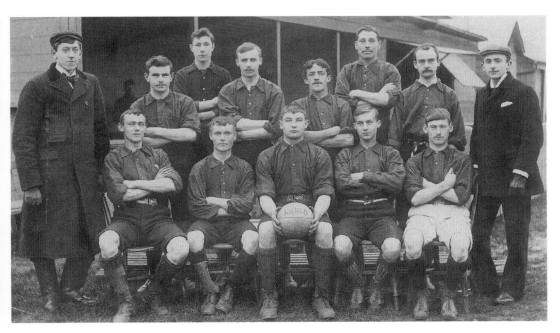

Littlehampton Football Club 1895-96. The coaches were G.E. Redman (far left) and P. Briggs (far right). From left to right, back row: J. Handscomb, W. Wilson. Middle row: W.G. Sandell, Taverner, M. Ive, J. Langrish. Bottom row: J. Piper, T. Newell, G.R. Wadham, R.A. Hale, W. Coddy.

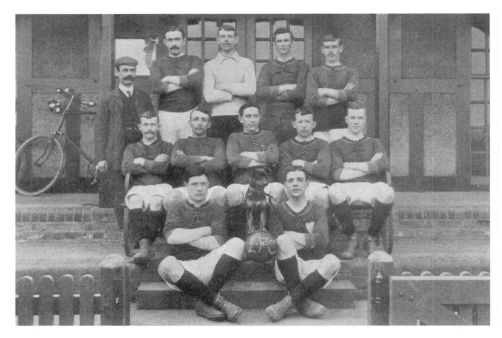

The 1906–07 Football Team for Littlehampton as photographed by F.W. Spry for *Lloyds News*. From left to right, back row: F. Rose, E. Sewell, D. Carpenter, R. Linfield, S. Tate. Second row: G. Creese, G. Batchelor, A. Holland, G. Price, H. Swift. Front row: Waterhouse, H. Woolven.

Littlehampton Rugby XV in 1923. They are pictured before playing the United Services on 15 December. The rugby club was made up of the young gentlemen who attended a tutoring establishment at 20 South Terrace in the 1870s. Littlehampton has not had a rugby club since the 1930s.

Local schoolchildren dancing around the maypole on May Day in the early 1900s. The maypole is a traditional English-village pastime, where a local gentleman would 'grant' a tree to the community. The poles were usually painted and decorated with ribbons, which the children would hold on to whilst dancing around the pole.

Bottle fishing at a summer fête in the 1930s. The whole town would come together to take part in traditional activities such as bottle fishing, apple bobbing and Morris dancing.

A contest of tug-of-war in 1902. The tradition of testing each other's strength and skill goes back to ancient times. At the courts of the Chinese emperors, teams were specifically trained for tug-of-war tournaments. It became an organised sport at the end of the nineteenth century when clubs were created.

Mothers taking part in a game of tug-of-war on Coronation Day in 1953, in Beaconsfield Road, Wick. Tug-of-war contests were once part of the Olympic programme up until 1920. Great Britain established a tug-of-war association in 1958 and it remains a popular village sport at local festivities.

Children enjoying a sack race to celebrate the Coronation of Queen Elizabeth II in 1953.

Littlehampton Cricket Club in the 1930s. There has been a local cricket club in Littlehampton since 1851, but the earliest record of a cricket match is from 2 July 1802, between Storrington and the Gentleman of Sussex. The local cricket team used to play their matches on Littlehampton Common in the late 1800s, but in 1872 they received notice from the Arundel Estate Office that the pitch was no longer available for their use. They subsequently moved their games to the field at the rear of Selbourne Road which became Littlehampton's first sports field.

Four gentlemen enjoying a game of bowls the early 1930s. Third from the right is Mr Walter Whyman.

Connaught Road Bowling Green, c. 1912. Connaught Bowling Club was the first bowling club in Littlehampton. It no longer exists as it was covered by Franciscan Way forty years ago.

Gentleman enjoying a round of golf at Littlehampton Golf Links. The golf club was formed on 16 February 1889 after a meeting at Terminus Hotel, and started with twenty-five members. It was originally a nine-hole course, which became an eighteen-hole course in 1893.

The Golf Links located on the west bank of the river Arun attracted many famous golfers such as Field Marshall Earl Hague and the future King George VI pictured here. Access to the Golf Links was via a rowboat ferry across the river Arun from Pier Road. Two local boatmen known as Peachy and Jimmy operated the ferry, charging 1d one way, and 2d for a return trip.

A view of the official opening of Littlehampton Sports Field in 1897. The sports field was generously donated to the town by the Duke of Norfolk who was the guest of honour at the opening ceremony. Prior to the gift of the sports field home matches for the rugby and football teams were usually played in 'Skinner's field', the meadow that was opposite Norfolk Place.

eight

Disasters!

R THE GALE - LITTLEHAMPTON

~ LITTLEHAMPTON, SEPT. 10 - 1933 ~

The steam ship *Mungret* stranded on the bank of the river Arun on 10 September 1933. She was built in a Dublin shipyard in 1912 and weighed 515 tonnes. The ship was originally known as the *Sligo* and belonged to the Limerick Steam Ship Co. She was used as a coastal trading vessel.

The steam ship *Dagfrid* run aground at Littlehampton on 25 October 1924. The cargo is Baltic timber imported from Scandinavia.

The yacht *Skylark* in difficulties by the mouth of the river Arun on 7 July 1913. In 1735 two piers were built to stop the entrance of the river Arun from silting up. The harbour mouth was deepened at a cost of £20,000 in 1825.

A steamroller in difficulties on 8 January 1914. The front roller has disappeared into a hole in Howard's Place. The steamroller was made at the workshops of James Penfold Ltd in Arundel.

Above: Dance Pavilion destroyed by fire on 8 July 1928. It was located at the end of Banjo Road alongside a bandstand, café and sunken gardens which were built in 1905. The Dance Pavilion was built in 1924 and could accommodate 500 dancers or 1,500 listeners. After the fire, the building was rebuilt by J. Lindfields & Sons and reopened in August 1928. All the buildings were demolished in 1968.

Left: Aftermath of a fire at the Electric Palace Cinema on 14 August 1922. The picture screen was shattered by the force of the explosion. The Electric Palace Cinema was situated in Terminus Road. It had previously been the Terminus Theatre and a skating rink. In 1931 it became the Regent Cinema.

Opposite above: Football stand at the sports field destroyed by fire on 4 December 1920. The stand was built in the 1890s. It was the home for many football teams over the years.

Straw on fire in Duke Street on 3 October 1908. The fire started in Constable's Brewery stables and coal stores. Luckily it was caught in time and did not cause much damage.

The Ship & Anchor Inn and Humphrey Brown Motor Launch Works flooded on River Road in June 1924. This was a wet year with more than 13in of rain falling during the summer.

High tide at the Arun View pub and Chain Ferry on 31 October 1905. The tide would regularly flood this part of the town.

Floods at the bus depot in East Street on 4 June 1929. Parts of the town were flooded after a summer gale caused the river Arun to break its banks.

River Road flooded on 4 June 1929. An 80mph gale hit Sussex, causing many seaside towns to be damaged or flooded.

Wrecked locomotive at Littlehampton Station on 4 August 1920. In the foreground, station master Edward Tanner, station master from 1895 until his retirement in 1922, is discussing details of the accident. The original Littlehampton Station was built in 1863 and demolished in 1938.

Crowds gather in Albert Road to observe the damage. There were thirty passengers on board the train of whom thirteen suffered minor injuries. The locomotive driver and fireman escaped injury by jumping from the footplate just before the collision occurred. Luckily there were no deaths.

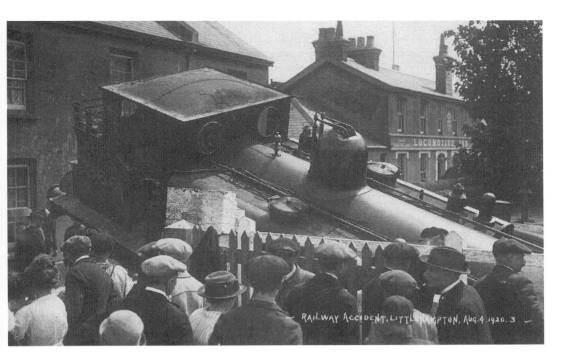

Railway accident at Littlehampton Station. A train consisting of eight carriages and Engine No. 360 (Type 0-4-2) travelling from Ford Junction Station crashed through the buffers and station wall.

A group of railway workers involved in the clearing-up operation are inspecting the damage. The accident was caused by the failure of the Westinghouse air brake and human error.

Littlehampton Golf Links club house flooded after a storm on 23 March 1913. The original club house was built in 1894 but was unfortunately burnt down in 1985.

Aftermath of destruction of the caddy's house. The original golf course was set among the sand dunes and proved an instant hit with golfers due to its remoteness.

Workmen repairing the damage done by the storm. The Golf Links were flooded after the river Arun burst its banks during a storm on the night of 22 March 1913.

Clearing the water from the flooded Golf Links.

South Terrace covered in snow on 30 December 1908. The Beach Hotel can be seen in the background. From December 1908 until March 1909, Sussex was hit by one of the worst snow blizzards since 1881.

Snow in Beach Road on 30 December 1908. Many towns and businesses in Sussex were almost cut off or brought to a standstill during this period of severe weather. The county would not experience such snow storms again until the winter of 1962-63.

Duke Street under snow on 30 December 1908. The Globe Inn was located at 4 Duke Street. It was established in 1866 and was owned by Robert Richards. He had been a beer retailer in the town since 1858.

Fitzalan Road in snow on 30 December 1908. The temperature plunged to an average of 4.5 degrees Celsius during that winter. It was in the winter of 1895 that the lowest ever temperature of 27.2 degrees Celcius was recorded in Britain.

Above: Outside The Rose & Crown public house on River Road after snowfall on 29 December 1908.

Left: East Beach and pier frozen over on 23 January 1907. The next occasion when the sea froze over at Littlehampton was in the winter of 1962-63.

Opposite above: Littlehampton East Beach and Sea frozen on the 23 January 1907. The pier and Pepper Pot Lighthouse can be seen in the background. Several feet of snow fell across Sussex during this particular winter.

LITTLEHAMPTON PARADE, MARCH 5. 1912.

Damage to the promenade after a storm on 5 March 1912. The coast of Sussex was hit by a severe gale in March 1912, causing damage to many seaside resorts.

Planks from smashed beach huts on the promenade after a gale on 2 June 1938. The Pavilion Café and big dipper at Butlins Amusement Park are in the background.

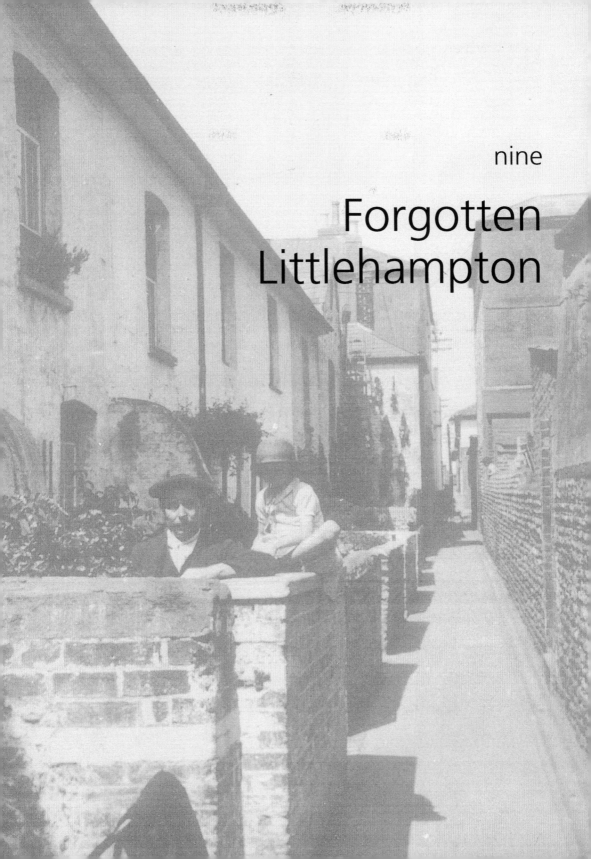

nine

Forgotten
Littlehampton

Anchor Cottages in Wick Street, *c.* 1900. This thatched dwelling was built in 1719.

Opposite above: Pound Cottage in East Street, *c.*1890. The cottage was demolished in the 1920s.

Opposite below: Hazelwood Cottages in the 1920s. These cottages stood on the site now occupied by Woolworths. They replaced a row of thatched dwellings which burnt down in 1868.

Hampton Court, *c.* 1920. This row of cottages dates from 1796 and was located between Terminus Road and River Road. It was demolished in 1950.

Maud Burtenshaw walking through Hampton Court. The Burtenshaws were a local fishing family in the early twentieth century.

The Arun Mill and amusement arcade, *c.* 1920. Built in 1831 by Henry Martin of Bognor Regis, the mill ceased to function in 1913. The adjoining amusements were opened in 1912 by Harry Joseph who purchased the site after winning the London Palladium's Pierrot Contest. His kursaal was a combined Pierrot theatre and fun house but sadly fell into decline, finally becoming penny arcade. In the early 1930s the building was demolished by Billy Butlin who acquired the site for his amusement park. The mill itself was demolished in 1932.

Above: Littlehampton Mill and Old Coastguard Cottages, *c.* 1890. This row of houses was built between 1843 and 1850. It was used to provide accommodation for men who worked as coastguards in the town.

Left: Pepper Pot Lighthouse in 1910. This stood at the entrance to the port and was one of a pair of lighthouses affectionately known as the Salt and Pepper Pots. Both were demolished during the Second World War.

Opposite above: Mewsbrook Swamp in 1935. This marshy area located between Littlehampton and Rustington was developed into the Mewsbrook Pleasure Grounds in the late 1930s and opened to the public in 1939.

Manor House and the town pump in 1932. The pump which stood outside the Manor House used to provide water to the people of Littlehampton. It was also where the local Methodist group would hold their open-air meetings. It was removed in 1932. The Manor House was built sometime between 1820 and 1830 on the site of Manor Farm.

Right: The Olympic Hall, built by Linfield & Sons in 1910, started life as a skating rink. In 1912 it became the Empire Theatre and by 1920 it was the Palladium Cinema. It was demolished in the 1990s.

Below: Interior of The Olympic Hall. This shot was taken during the building's life as a theatre. You can see the decorated stage ready for a production.

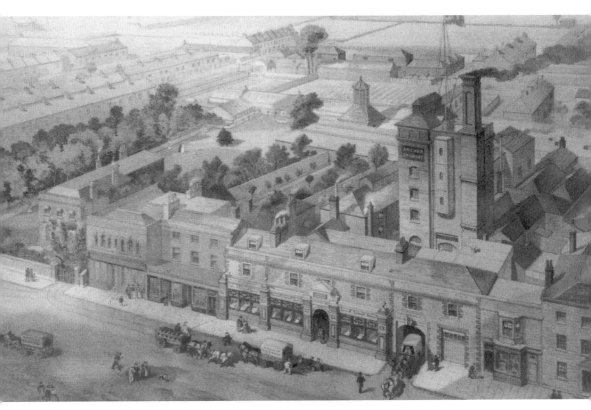

The Anchor Brewery was owned by the brewing family, the Constables. John Constable acquired the building in 1853, and considerably extended it in 1871 with a tall tower block and square chimney which was visible for miles. Whilst Thomas, John's brother, was in charge of the business it became the second largest employer in Littlehampton. During the Second World War the tower block lost its chimney and in 1972 the whole site was demolished.

Corney's Tea Garden, c. 1920. Owned by the Corney family in the early twentieth century, these tea gardens were a favourite place for locals to visit in the small hamlet of Toddington.

A 1910 guidebook featured a delightful advertisement for the Corney's Tea Garden offering, 'Tea or hot water provided in meadow, garden or orchard. Cut flowers, fruit and vegetables. Buses every ½ hour. swings, see-saw, stoolball etc'.

Bungalow Tea Rooms in 1923. Located in Beach Road, this café was one of the most popular in Littlehampton. It advertised 'Dainty teas and suppers' and on a Tuesday evening from 8 p.m. to 11 p.m. dancing would take place.

Beach Hotel and Jubilee Fountain, c. 1905. This fountain, which stood in the park opposite the Beach Hotel, was erected to mark the Coronation of King Edward VII in 1902. Unfortunately the fountain was dismantled during the Second World War.

The large elm tree was situated at the junction of Surrey Street and the High Street. This tree was the gathering point of the village and was where the daily distribution of mail took place. Frank Broad, the mail carrier, and his donkey used to collect the letters and packages from the coach at Arundel and take position under the tree as the villagers came to collect their post. On Fair days a lady known as the 'lucky bag woman' used to sit under the shade of the branches with a bag of treats and surprises for the local children. Also, once a year a 'mock mayor' was appointed under this majestic elm, a position subject to much joviality. The tree was sadly cut down in March 1820.

Opposite above: Parish church, *c.* 1820. This image was featured in *The Gentleman's Magazine* in June 1834. The view is of the church, located in Church Street, before its rebuilding in 1826. It is believed that a church has been on this site since Saxon times.

Opposite below: This farmyard was located on the corner of Arundel Road and the High Street. The attached barn used to be a venue for theatrical performances. In 1859 the plot was leased from the Duke of Norfolk and the Congregational church was built on the site. Local builder Robert Bushby was in charge of the project and the foundation stone was laid by Samuel Morley, the MP for Bristol, who had helped secure the land. The construction was completed by October 1861.

~ OLD LITTLEHAMPTON ~
~ WHERE THE CONGREGATIONAL CHURCH NOW STANDS ~

Other local titles published by The History Press

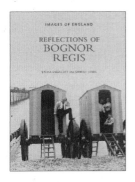

Bognor Regis

SYLVIA ENDACOTT AND SHIRLEY LEWIS

Bognor Regis today is a vibrant seaside resort. As well as boasting one of the oldest piers in Britain, the town is known for Billy Butlin and his impact on bringing bucket-loads of holiday makers to the resort. Visitors and residents old and new will enjoy seeing the people and the buildings over the centuries that have made Bognor Regis what it is today.

978 07524 4299 0

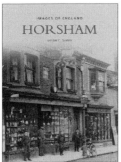

Horsham

SUSAN DJABRI

This collection of nearly 200 images, mostly drawn from the collections of Horsham Museum, and many never before published, provides a fascinating pictorial history of the town over the last two centuries. *Horsham* is a valuable pictorial record of the town's history, which will awaken nostalgic memories for some, while offering a unique glimpse of the past for others.

0 7524 3831 X

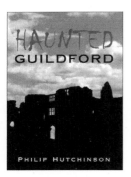

Haunted Guildford

PHILIP HUTCHINSON

Haunted Guildford contains a chilling range of ghostly accounts. From tales of a piano-playing spirit at Guildford Museum and a spectral monk who wanders up Friary Street, to stories of a poltergeist at the Three Pigeons public house and sightings of a ghostly woman on Whitmoor Common, this selection is sure to appeal to anyone interested in the supernatural history of the area.

0 7524 3826 3

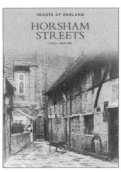

Horsham Streets

SYLVIA BARLOW

A thriving and bustling market town, Horsham is a place with a sense of its own identity. From its early origins it is well known for its sheep, cattle and corn markets. Many streets are covered, from the first streets named simply North, South, East and West to Belloc Close and Shelley Court after the famous poets who once lived around Horsham. This absorbing book captures Horsham's heritage and offers a unique glimpse into the town's past.

978 07524 4305 8

If you are interested in purchasing other books published by The History Press, or in case you have difficulty finding any of our books in your local bookshop, you can also place orders directly through our website

www.thehistorypress.co.uk